THE ULTIMATE BOOK OF
BEER
TRIVIA

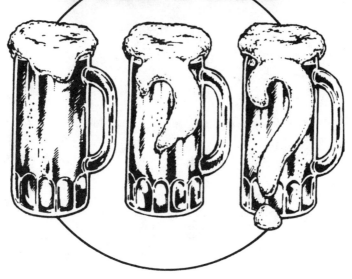

THE ULTIMATE BOOK OF

BEER TRIVIA

Bill Yenne and Tom Debolski

BLUEWOOD BOOKS

This edition produced and published in 1994
by Bluewood Books
A Division of The Siyeh Group, Inc.
PO Box 460313
San Francisco, CA 94146

ISBN 0-912517-02-6

Printed in the USA

About the authors:
Bill Yenne has hosted many beer
tastings, and has written many articles and
several books on beer and brewing
history. Among his books are *Beers of
North America, Beers of the World* and
Beer Labels of the World.
Tom Debolski is an accomplished
home brewer who is dedicated to
extolling the virtues opaque beer.

CONTENTS

INTRODUCTION

Welcome to *The Ultimate Book of Beer Trivia*. It's designed to provide hours of fun for you and your friends to enjoy over a few pints of your favorite brew.

The answers are on the back of the page that the question is on so they're easy to find, while at the same time they're out of sight so you won't be tempted to peek.

The book is organized into four sections so you can choose your topic. Home brewers and technical folks will like the section *Making Beer*, while history buffs will love *Legends and Lore*. Everybody will enjoy *Just Labels*, *Slogans and Advertising* and *People Who Made Beer Famous* because these are the kinds of minute bits of information that tend to stick in the back of our minds. What *was* the beer that made Milwaukee famous?

The Ultimate Book of Beer Trivia is designed so that you can enjoy it alone in the comfort of your own home or with several friends at your favorite neighborhood pub. You might even want to organize teams and invite everyone in your sorority, on your block or from your wing at the retirement villa to join in the fun!

So what are you waiting for? Call up some friends, pick up a six pack and see who knows the Latvian word for beer or which beer label features the world's oldest registered trademark!

Cheers!

HOW TO PLAY

By yourself:

A. Pour yourself a glass of your favorite beer.

B. Choose one or more of the five categories.

C. On a sheet of paper, answer the questions on the first right-hand page.

D. Check your answers on the following left-hand page. Give yourself one point for each correct answer. Keep score on a separate sheet of paper. Some questions have more than one part. Each part is worth one point.

E. Repeat steps C and D with the next set of questions and answers.

F. When you've finished one category, go on to the next category.

G. Repeat step A as often as necessary. However, do not operate a motor vehicle if you repeat step A too often.

With a Friend or Two:

A. Pour a glass of beer for each player.

B. Choose one or more of the five categories.

C. Ask one of the other players to answer all of the questions on the first right-hand page, or ask each player one by one.

D. Check the answers on the following left-hand page. Give each player one point for each correct answer. Keep score on a sheet of paper. Some questions have more than one part. Each part is worth one point.

E. Repeat steps C and D with the next set of questions and answers. The second player asks the third if there are three people, or the first player if there are just two of you.

F. When you've finished one category, go on to the next category.

G. Repeat step A as often as necessary. However, do not operate a motor vehicle if you repeat step A too often.

With a Quizmaster
(for groups of four or more):

A. Pour a glass of beer for everyone, or order a couple of pitchers. Pick an adequate number of designated drivers before you start the quiz.

B. Choose one or more of the five categories.

C. The Quizmaster asks a question and picks the first person to raise a hand to answer. If two or more people raise their hands, the Quizmaster picks the one who hasn't answered lately. *Important:* Saying an answer out loud without being called on automatically disqualifies that answer. Multiple part questions may be divided among players or asked separately.

D. The Quizmaster will reveal the answers on the following left-hand page and award one point for each correct answer. A designated scorekeeper will keep score on a piece of paper or a chalkboard. Some questions have more than one part. Each part is worth one point.

E. Repeat steps C and D with each question and answer.

F. When you've finished one category, go on to the next category.

G. Repeat step A as often as necessary. However, do not operate a motor vehicle if you repeat step A too often.

With Teams (for groups of four or more):

A. Pour a glass of beer for everyone, or order a couple of pitchers. Pick an adequate number of designated drivers before you start the quiz.

B. Select the players for each team and choose one or more of the five categories.

C. The teams will take turns asking the questions on the right-hand pages. Multiple part questions may be divided between players or asked separately.

D. A neutral scorekeeper or a trusted member of each team will check the answers on the following left-hand page and award one point for each correct answer. The scorekeeper will keep score on a piece of paper or a chalkboard. Some questions have more than one part. Each part is worth one point.

E. Repeat steps C and D with each question and answer.

F. When you've finished one category, go on to the next category.

G. Repeat step A as often as necessary. However, do not operate a motor vehicle if you repeat step A too often.

Note: When a question has a large number of possible answers (such as a list of beer brands with bears on the label), the person asking the question may ask for as many as seem appropriate. We have suggested "three or more," but the quizmaster may choose to ask for one, three or as many as are on the list. A point is assigned for each correct answer. In all these cases, we've listed all the answers that we could think of, but there may very well be others that we have *not* included. If a player names one of these and can *prove it* to the satisfaction of the Quizmaster, then that answer also counts.

Data listed in parentheses is optional and is included for the sake of information. It may be used for additional points at the descretion of the players, or as a tie-breaker at the descretion of the Quizmaster. In the case of dates from before the twentieth century, the Quizmaster may wish to allow five or ten years of latitude.

In cases of disagreement over interpretation, the Quizmaster's ruling is final.

1.
SLOGANS & ADVERTISING

1.01 What beer made Milwaukee famous?

1.02 Who brews it?

1.03 What American beer is known as the "Silver Bullet"?

1.04 What brand is today known as the "King of Beers"? **1.05** Why?

1.06 Budweiser is now known as the "King of Beers." Name three or more other beers that were previously known as the "King of Beers."

1.07 Budweiser is known as the "King of Beers." "The Beer of Kings" is the slogan associated with what beer? **1.08** Who brews it?

1.09 What is "America's Fire Brewed Beer"? **1.10** Who brews it?

1.11 Why do bock beers brewed in Germany, the United States and elsewhere have a goat on the label?

(answers on the following page)

13

ANSWERS TO THE QUESTIONS ON PAGE 13:

1.01 Schlitz. **1.02** Stroh Brewery Company. Stroh operates brewing plants in St Paul, MN; Allentown, PA; Longview, TX; Memphis, TN; Van Nuys, CA; and Winston-Salem, NC, but *not* in Milwaukee.

1.03 Coors Light.

1.04 Budweiser, brewed by Anheuser Busch (St Louis, MO and elsewhere). **1.05** It is the largest-selling single beer brand in the world.

1.06 • Bohemian—American Brewing (St Louis, MO).
 • Imperial Beer—Beadle's & Woerz (New York, NY).
 • Little Kings Cream Ale—Hudepohl-Schoenling (Cincinnati, OH).
 • Anheuser Busch's Michelob was once known as the "King of Draft Beers."
 Other answers admissible with proof

1.07 Tuborg. **1.08** Tuborg Brewery, part of the Carlsberg Group (Denmark) and under license in the United States by Heileman.

1.09 Stroh's. **1.10** Stroh Brewery Company (headquartered in Detroit, MI, with brewing in Texas, California, Tennessee and North Carolina).

1.11 Because "bock" is also the German word for goat.

1.12 What brewing company has the first trademark to be registered in Britain (and possibly in the world)? **1.13** What is that trademark?

1.14 "Just Say OV" is the slogan associated with what beer?
1.15 Who brews it?

1.16 What is the man's first name most commonly used in the naming of English pubs? **1.17** Why?

1.18 "The Brew is True" is the slogan associated with what beer?
1.19 Who brews it?

1.20 Name three beers that are or were named after hats.

(answers on the following page)

ANSWERS TO THE QUESTIONS ON PAGE 15:

1.12 Bass & Company (Burton-upon-Trent, England).
1.13 A red triangle.

1.14 Old Vienna. **1.15** It is brewed not in Vienna, Austria, or Vienna, Virginia, but in Canada by Molson Breweries.

1.16 George. **1.17** Because St George is the patron saint of England, and/or there have been six English kings with that name.

1.18 Connors.
1.19 Connors Brewing (Mississauga, Ontario, Canada).

1.20 • Brown Derby Lager—General Brewing (Tumwater, WA).
  • Top Hat Beer—Hudepohl-Schoenling (Cincinnati, OH).
  • Red Cap Ale—Carling-O'Keefe, now part of Molson Breweries (Canada).
  Other answers admissible with proof

1.21 What brewery launched a long-running ad campaign in the 1930s and 1940s to convince women that beer was "dietetically non-fattening"?

1.22 Many mass market beer brands in the United States have used scantily clad women and swimsuit models in their advertising. What brewing company in the United Kingdom consistently used pin-up girls on their labels for many years before they bowed to the tide of "political correctness"?

1.23 What beer brand was known in the 1930s and 1940s as the "Pride of Newark" (PON) or "A Rhapsody in Brew"?

(answers on the following page)

ANSWERS TO THE QUESTIONS ON PAGE 17:

1.21 Acme Brewing (San Francisco and Los Angeles, CA).

1.22 Tennent's Caledonian Brewery (Glasgow, Scotland).

1.23 Feigenspan (Newark, NJ).

1.24 What beer was packaged in camouflage-colored cans during World War II?

1.25 "Iron City Beer" is the official beer of what United States city?

1.26 "Great taste makes it a great beer" was a slogan associated with what beer?

1.27 What is the "national beer" of Texas? **1.28** Who brews it?

1.29 With which beer brand is this character associated?

1.30 Who brews it?

(answers on the following page)

ANSWERS TO THE QUESTIONS ON PAGE 19:

1.24 Schaefer (New York, NY).

1.25 Pittsburgh, PA.

1.26 Carling Black Label.

1.27 Lone Star.

1.28 G. Heileman Brewing (San Antonio, TX).

1.29 Cincinnati Cream ("The Famous Cinci").

1.30 Molson Breweries (Canada).

1.31 Which beer brand made the following silly offer in its advertising in the early 1990s: "Free Foam with Purchase"?
1.32 Who brewed it?

1.33 "Makes it Fun to be Thirsty" was a slogan associated with what beer? **1.34** Who brewed it?

1.35 Name three or more American brewing companies with one-syllable names ending in the letter "z."

1.36 "Always Pick a Nick" is the slogan associated with what beer?
1.37 Who brews it?

1.38 Name three or more beer brands—*not* breweries— that are named after saints.
1.39 Name the brewer of each brand.

1.40 "The Beer Drinker's Beer" was the confident slogan associated with what beer? **1.41** Who brewed it?

(answers on the following page)

ANSWERS TO THE QUESTIONS ON PAGE 21:

1.31 Augsburger. **1.32** Stroh Brewery Company.

1.33 Bub's Beer. **1.34** Walter Brewing (Eau Claire, WI).

1.35 • Blatz (Milwaukee, WI).
  • Blitz (Portland, OR).
  • Goetz (St. Joseph, MO).
  • Gretz (Philadelphia, PA).
  • Schlitz (Milwaukee, WI).
  • Stolz—International Brewing (Covington, KY).
  • Storz (Omaha, NE).
    Other answers admissible with proof

1.36 Kinnikinick Ale.
1.37 Twenty Tank Brewery (San Francisco, CA).

1.38 / 1.39 • St. Hubertus—Kuehtreiber Brewery (Laa, Austria).
  • St. Leonard—Saingt Brewery (Lille, France).
  • St. Sixtus—St. Bernardus Brewery (Watou, Belgium).
  • San Miguel—San Miguel Brewery (Manila, Philippines).
  • St. Sebastian—Sterkens-Meer Brewery (Hoogstraten, Belgium).
  • St. Stan's—Stanislaus Brewing (Modesto, CA).
    Other answers admissible with proof

1.40 Fort Schyler Lager. **1.41** FX Matt Brewing (Utica, NY).

1.42 / 1.43 / 1.44 In 1992, a midwestern brewing company used its leading brand in an advertising campaign to protect endangered species found 3,000 miles away in the mountain West of the United States and Canada. Name the company, the brand and the endangered species.

1.45 What well-known politician congratulated the brewing company referred to in 1.42 in the *Congressional Record* on June 7, 1993?

1.46 What beer was traditionally known as "The Champagne of Bottled Beer"? **1.47** Who brews it?

1.48 Today, nearly everyone knows what a fax machine is, and many of us have used one. In what country is Faxe a brand of beer?

1.49 "From the Country of 1100 Springs" was a slogan associated with what beer? **1.50** Who brewed it?

1.51 What United States airline offered a beer called "Brew 747" on its Hawaii-bound flights in the 1970s?

1.52 "Ask the Boy for the Less Filling Beer" was the slogan associated with what beer? **1.53** Who brewed it?

1.54 "It Takes a Tough Brewmaster to Make a Tender Beer" was a slogan associated with what beer? **1.55** Who brewed it?

1.56 Describe the appearance of the fictional brewmaster that appeared in the advertising, for the beer referred to in 1.54.

(answers on the following page)

ANSWERS TO THE QUESTIONS ON PAGE 23:

1.42 Hudepohl-Schoenling (Cincinnati, OH).
1.43 Little Kings Cream Ale. **1.44** Grizzly bear (*ursus arctos*).

1.45 Vice president Al Gore.

1.46 Miller High Life. **1.47** Miller Brewing (Milwaukee, WI).

1.48 Denmark. (The Faxe Brewery is located in Fakse on the east coast, south of Copenhagen.)

1.49 Pearl Lager. **1.50** Pearl Brewing (San Antonio, TX).

1.51 United Air Lines.

1.52 Knickerbocker Beer.
1.53 Jacob Ruppert Brewing (New York, NY).

1.54 Rainier. **1.55** Rainier Brewing (Seattle, WA).

1.56 The fictional brewmaster was bald with a black handlebar mustache.

1.57 "Save the Caps to Beat the Japs" was the slogan used during World War II to promote the reycling of the bottle caps from what beer?
1.58 Who brewed it?

1.59 Samuel Smith's Old Brewery in Yorkshire in England brews a beer called Taddy Porter. What does "Taddy" mean?

1.60 "The Choicest Product of the Brewer's Art" was a slogan associated with what beer? **1.61** Who brewed it?

1.62 "The Brew That Grew with the Great Northwest" was a slogan associated with what beer? **1.63** Who brewed it? 1.64Where?

(answers on the following page)

ANSWERS TO THE QUESTIONS ON PAGE 25:

1.57 Regal Pale Ale. **1.58** Regal Brewing (Detroit, MI).

1.59 Taddy is short for Tadcaster, which is the town in Yorkshire where the brewery is located.

1.60 Falstaff. **1.61** Falstaff Brewing (Fort Wayne, IN).

1.62 Schmidt. **1.63** Jacob Schmidt Brewing. **1.64** St Paul, MN.

1.65 "It's Registered Pure" was a slogan associated with what beer?
1.66 Who brews it?

1.67 Who brewed a product with the intriguing name "Time Saver Beer"?

1.68 "America's Largest Selling Ale" was a slogan associated with what beer during its heyday?

1.69 Who brewed the beer referred to in 1.68 originally? **1.70** Who brews it now?

"YOU'LL NEVER MISS THE WATER"

(answers on the following page)

ANSWERS TO THE QUESTIONS ON PAGE 27:

1.65 Wiedemann. **1.66** G. Heileman (La Crosse, WI).

1.67 Royal Brewery (New Orleans, LA), circa 1975.

1.68 Ballantine Ale. **1.69** Ballantine Brewing (New York, NY).

1.70 Falstaff Brewing (Fort Wayne, IN).

1.71 "The Beer That is Beer" was probably the most straight-forward slogan ever used to sell beer or any other product. At least nobody ever questioned it. It was used to identify what specific beer?
1.72 Who brewed it?

1.73 "The Beer That's Liquid Food" was a slogan associated with what beer? **1.74** Who brewed it?

1.75 What American beer is advertised as having been "beechwood aged"? **1.76** Who brews it?

1.77 What beer claimed to "Win Cheers in Any League"?
1.78 Who brewed it?

1.79 What does the suffix "ator" mean when it is attached to the brand name of a German-style beer?

Name the brewery that produces each of the following famous doppelbock beers:

1.80 Animator.   **1.83** Delicator.   **1.87** Optimator.

1.81 Apostulator.   **1.84** Kulminator.   **1.88** Salvator.

1.82 Celebrator.   **1.85** Luxator.   **1.89** Triumphator.

                           1.86 Maximator.

(answers on the following page)

ANSWERS TO THE QUESTIONS ON PAGE 29:

1.71 Walter's. **1.72** Hibernia Brewing (formerly Walter Brewing, Eau Claire, WI).

1.73 High Grade Beer. **1.74** Brewed circa 1912 by Galveston Brewing (Galveston, TX).

1.75 Budweiser. **1.76** Anheuser Busch (St Louis, MO and other locations).

1.77 Duquesne Pilsner. **1.78** Duquesne Brewing (Pittsburgh, PA).

1.79 It signifies that the beer is a doppelbock (double bock), a version of bock beer (rich, dark lager) with a high alcohol content. However, Terminator, brewed by the McMenamin Brothers in Oregon, is listed as a stout.

1.80 Animator—Hacker-Pschorr (Munich, Germany).
1.81 Apostulator—Eichbaum (Mannheim, Germany).
1.82 Celebrator—Ayinger (Aying, Germany).
1.83 Delicator—Hofbrauhaus Munich (Munich, Germany).
1.84 Kulminator—Erste Kulmbacher Union (EKU) (Kulmbach, Germany).
1.85 Luxator—Mousel (Luxembourg).
1.86 Maximator—Augustiner (Munich, Germany).
1.87 Optimator—Spaten-Franziskaner (Munich, Germany).
1.88 Salvator—Paulaner-Thomasbrau (Munich, Germany).
1.89 Triumphator—Lowenbrau (Munich, Germany).

1.90 With what beer is the character pictured at the right associated?

1.91 According to the slogan, what "land" is he and his beer from?

Name the language or languages, in which each of the following is the word for "beer":

1.92 Alus.

1.93 Bier.

1.94 Bière.

1.95 Cerveja.

1.96 Cerveza.

1.97 Olut.

1.98 Pivo.

1.99 Piwo.

1.100 What beer is known by the slogan "Time for a Tiger"?

1.101 Who brews it?

(answers on the following page)

ANSWERS TO THE QUESTIONS ON PAGE 31:

1.90 Hamm's.

1.91 "The Land of Sky Blue Waters" (St Paul, MN).

1.92 Alus—Latvian.

1.93 Bier—German, Dutch or Flemish.

1.94 Bière—French.

1.95 Cerveja—Portuguese.

1.96 Cerveza—Spanish.

1.97 Olut—Finnish.

1.98 Pivo—Czech or Russian.

1.99 Piwo—Polish.

1.100 Tiger Beer.

1.101 Asia Pacific Brewery (formerly Malayan Breweries, Ltd., Singapore).

1.102 Twelve-ounce bottles are the size most commonly used by American brewers. What American beer was, for most of its history, sold exclusively in 7-ounce bottles? **1.103** Who brews it?

1.104 "Born in the Land of Sky Blue Waters" is the slogan associated with what beer? **1.105** Who brews it?

In Canada, the principle brand of each of the major brewing companies is associated with a particular color. Name the brewer and its product that are known by each of these colors:
1.106 Gold
1.107 Blue
1.108 Black.

1.109 "Pocono Mountain Water Makes the Difference" is the slogan associated with what beer? **1.110** Who brews it?

1.111 Name three or more beer brands or breweries named for mountains or mountain ranges. Not applicable are brands that simply have pictures of mountains on their labels.

1.112 "It's the Water" is the slogan associated with what beer?
1.113 Who brews it?

1.114 "Who Wants the Handsome Waiter?" is the slogan associated with what beer? **1.115** Who brews it?

(answers on the following page)

ANSWERS TO THE QUESTIONS ON PAGE 33:

1.102 Little Kings Cream Ale. **1.103** Hudepohl-Schoenling (Cincinnati, OH).

1.104 Hamm's. **1.105** Theodore Hamm Brewing, now part of Pabst Brewing (St. Paul, MN).

1.106 Molson Golden.
1.107 Labatt's Blue.
1.108 Carling Black Label.

1.109 Gibbons Famous Lager Beer. **1.110** Gibbons Brewery, aka the Lion (Wilkes Barre, PA).

1.111 • Alpine—Moosehead (New Brunswick, Canada).
   • Black Mountain Gold—Crazy Ed's (Cave Creek, AZ).
   • Devil Mountain Brewery (Walnut Creek, CA).
   • Mt. Hood Brewing Company (Government Camp, OR).
   • Mt. Tam Pale Ale—Marin Brewing (Larkspur, CA).
   • Rainier—Rainier Brewing (Seattle, WA).
   • Red Mountain—Birmingham Brewery (Birmingham, AL).
   • Rockies Brewing Company (Boulder, CA).
   • Rocky Light—Rocky Mountain (Alberta, Canada).
   • Sierra Nevada Brewing (Chico, CA).
   • Spanish Peaks Brewery (Bozeman, MT).
   • Table Rock Brewpub (Boise, ID).
   • Various Wasatch beers—Schirf Brewing (Park City, UT).
   Other answers admissible with proof.

1.112 Olympia. **1.113** Pabst Brewing (Tumwater, WA).

1.114 Cincinnati Cream ("The Famous Cinci").
1.115 Molson Breweries (Canada).

1.116 Name three or more beer brands that have a nautical theme to their names. **1.117** Name the brewer of each.

1.118 "Simply Harmless" was the reassuring, but nonetheless ominous, slogan associated with what beer? **1.119** Where was it brewed?

1.120 Why was this beer considered to be "Simply Harmless"?

(answers on the following page)

ANSWERS TO THE QUESTIONS ON PAGE 35:

1.116 / 1.117
- Anchor Beer—Archipelago Brewery (Singapore).
- Anchor Steam Beer—Anchor Brewing (San Francisco, CA).
- Old Foghorn—Anchor Brewing (San Francisco, CA).
- Full Sail Ale—Hood River Brewing (Hood River, OR).
- Bosun's Black, Clipper Gold, Flagship Red Ale, Jolly Roger Christmas Ale, Navigator Dark, Nightwatch Ale and Windjammer Dark—Maritime Pacific Brewing (Seattle, WA).
- Harpoon Ale—Massachusetts Bay Brewing (Boston, MA).
- Kapitain—Pivovary Severoceske (Severoceske, Czechoslovakia).
- Lighthouse—Santa Cruz Brewing (Santa Cruz, CA).
- Schooner—Oland Breweries (Halifax, Nova Scotia, Canada).
  Other answers admissible with proof

1.118 East Side Temperance Beer. **1.119** Brewed in Los Angeles, CA (circa 1910).

1.120 East Side Temperance Beer contained less than 2 percent alcohol.

2.
JUST LABELS

Note: In some cases there are microbrewed beers with *names* that fit the category but they don't count unless they have the appropriate *labels*.

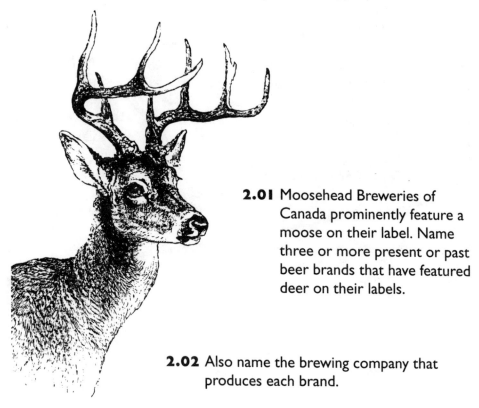

2.01 Moosehead Breweries of Canada prominently feature a moose on their label. Name three or more present or past beer brands that have featured deer on their labels.

2.02 Also name the brewing company that produces each brand.

2.03 The label of what American beer depicts a horseshoe with the words "Good Luck" inscribed on it? **2.04** Who brews it?

(answers on the following page)

ANSWERS TO THE QUESTIONS ON PAGE 39:

2.01 / 2.02
- Stag Beer—G. Heileman Brewing (Milwaukee, WI).
- Hudepohl Gold Lager—Hudepohl-Schoenling (Cincinnati, OH).
- Jackson Hole Draft Beer—Kessler Brewing (Helena, MT).
- Alexander Keith's India Pale Ale—Labatt (Halifax, Nova Scotia, Canada).
- Dominion Lager—Old Dominion Brewing (Ashborn, VA).
- Buckhorn Beer—Pabst Brewing (Milwaukee, WI).
- Deer Brand—August Schell Brewing (New Ulm, MN).
- Ulmer Braun Strong Beer—August Schell Brewing (New Ulm, MN).
- Entire line of products—Stoudt Brewing (Adamstown, PA).
- Stag Lager—Toohey's (Lidcombe, New South Wales, Australia).
- Entire line of products—Whitbread (London, England).
  Other answers admissible with proof

2.03 Olympia. **2.04** Pabst Brewing (Tumwater, WA).

2.05 Name two beer brands that feature a dog on their label.
2.06 Name the brewer of each.

2.07 What British beer, not among the above-mentioned, is known informally as "Dog"? **2.08** What related beer is known informally as "Pup"?

2.09 Name two beer brands that feature a parrot on their labels.
2.10 Who brews them?

2.11 Name a brewing company that features a badger on its label.
2.12 Where is it located?

2.13 Variations on what scene appeared on all seven beer cans of the "James Bond 007" series in the 1960s?
2.14 What American brewer brewed it?

2.15 Name a beer brand that features a seal on its label.
2.16 Who brews it?

(answers on the following page)

ANSWERS TO THE QUESTIONS ON PAGE 41:

2.05 / 2.06
- MacAndrew's—Caledonian Brewery (Scotland).
- Black Dog—Spanish Peaks (Bozeman, MT).
- Various products, if labelled, from the Flying Dog Brewpub (Aspen, CO).
  Other answers admissible with proof

2.07 Newcastle Brown Ale is known to the locals of Newcastle, England as "Dog." **2.08** Newcastle Lager is called "Pup."

2.09 / 2.10
- Ara Beer—DeDolle Brewery (Esen, Belgium).
- South Pacific Lager—South Pacific (Papua, New Guinea).
  Other answers admissible with proof

2.11 Hall & Woodhouse. **2.12** Blandford, England.
Other answers admissible with proof

2.13 A London scene at different times of day, along with the face of a young woman. **2.14** The now defunct National Brewing Company (Phoenix, AZ).

2.15 Red Seal Ale. **2.16** North Coast Brewing (Fort Bragg, CA).
Other answers admissible with proof

2.17 Name a beer brand that features a hummingbird on its label. **2.18** Who brews it?

2.19 Name a beer brand that features a giraffe on its label. **2.20** Who brews it?

2.21 What do the initials ESB signify when they appear on a beer label, such as those of Fuller's ESB and Red Hook ESB?

2.22 What do the initials IPA signify when they appear on a beer label?

2.23 In what country did the the phrase identified with the initials IPA originate?

2.24 Name a beer brand that features a grizzly bear on its label. **2.25** Who brews it?

2.26 Name a beer brand that features a polar bear on its label. **2.27** Who brews it?

(answers on the following page)

ANSWERS TO THE QUESTIONS ON PAGE 43:

2.17 Red Nectar Ale. **2.18** Humboldt Brewing (Arcata, CA).
Other answers admissible with proof

2.19 Giraf Beer. **2.20** Albani Brewery (Odense, Denmark).
Other answers admissible with proof

2.21 Extra Special Bitter.

2.22 India Pale Ale.

2.23 England.

2.24 Grizzly Canadian Lager. **2.25** Amstel Brewery (Hamilton, Ontario, Canada).
Other answers admissible with proof

2.26 Grant's Weis Beer. **2.27** Yakima Brewing (Yakima, WA).
Other answers admissible with proof

2.28 Name three or more beer brands and/or breweries that name or picture a chicken or rooster on their labels.

2.29 What type of character did the Foster Brewing Company of Australia feature on the label of its stout in the 1890s? (*Hint:* it was *not* a shrimp on a barbie, and it was *not* Paul Hogan.)

2.30 Name three or more beer brands that feature crocodiles or alligators on their labels. **2.31** Name the brewer of each.

2.32 A bottle of pale ale from what well-known brewing company appears in Eduard Manet's 1882 painting *The Bar at the Folies-Bergeres?*

2.33 Name a discontinued beer brand that featured a cardinal on its label. **2.34** Who brewed it?

(answers on the following page)

ANSWERS TO THE QUESTIONS ON PAGE 45:

2.28 • Cock of the Rock Porter—Big Rock Brewery (Calgary, Alberta, Canada).
• Cold Cock Porter—Big Rock Brewery (Calgary, Alberta, Canada).
• Old Speckled Hen (name only)—Morland (Abingdon, England).
• All products brewed by Blue Ridge Brewing (Charlottesville, VA) feature a rooster on the label.
• Scananavian Easter beers often feature baby chicks.
Other answers admissible with proof

2.29 A harlequin.

2.30 / 2.31
• Razor Edge—J Boag & Son (Launceston, Tasmania, Australia).
• Xingu Black Beer—Cervejaria Cacador (Cacador, Brazil).
• Delirium Tremens—Huyghe (Ghent, Belgium).
• Ngok—SCBK (Brazzaville, Republic of the Congo).
• Mamba—Solibra (Abidjan, Ivory Coast).
Other answers admissible with proof

2.32 Bass & Company (Burton-upon-Trent, England).

2.33 Cardinal Beer. **2.34** Cardinal Brewing (Detroit, MI and St Charles, MO).
Other answers admissible with proof

2.35 What German brewery features a shovel on its labels?

2.36 Name three or more beer brands that have featured a hog or wild boar on their labels. **2.37** Name the brewer of each.

2.38 / 2.39 Name two breweries that feature a swan on their labels and as part of their logos and the cities where they are located.

2.40 With what beer is the character at right associated?

2.41 Name three beer brands that have featured a cat on their labels. **2.42** Name the brewer of each.

(answers on the following page)

ANSWERS TO THE QUESTIONS ON PAGE 47:

2.35 Spatenbrau (Munich, Germany).

2.36 / 2.37
- Premium Light Ale—Blitz-Weinhard (Portland, OR).
- Brick Premium Lager—Brick Brewing (Ontario, Canada).
- [The original label of] Erlanger—Dubuque Star Brewing (Dubuque, IA).
- The Hogshead Brewpub (Sacramento, CA) features one in its logo.
  Other answers admissible with proof

2.38 / 2.39
- Swan Brewery (Perth, Australia).
- Swan's Brewpub (Victoria, BC, Canada).
  Other answers admissible with proof

2.40 The Fischer brand of Brasserie du Pecheur (Schiltigheim, Alsace, France).

2.41 / 2.42
- Cat Tail Ale—Dead Cat Alley Brewing (Woodland, CA).
- Dead Cat Lager—Dead Cat Alley Brewing (Woodland, CA).
- Fat Cat Porter—Dead Cat Alley Brewing (Woodland, CA).
- Yperman—Leroy Brewing (Boezinge, Belgium).
  Other answers admissible with proof

2.43 Name three or more breweries whose brands feature a pelican on their labels. **2.44** Name the city where each is located.

2.45 Name a beer brand that features a rabbit on its label.
2.46 Who brews it?

2.47 Describe the unique gate of Carlsberg's Copenhagen brewery.

2.48 Carlsberg's unique Copenhagen gate is featured on the label of which of their products?

2.49 Name three beer brands or breweries that feature an elephant on their labels or logo. **2.50** Name the brewery of each.

(answers on the following page)

ANSWERS TO THE QUESTIONS ON PAGE 49:

2.43 / 2.44
- Golden Pacific (Emeryville, CA).
- Pelforth (Lille, France).
- Sarasota Brewing (Sarasota, FL).
- Seabright Brewery (Santa Cruz, CA).
  Other answers admissible with proof

2.45 Bos Keun. **2.46** De Dolle Brewery (Esen, Belgium).
Other answers admissible with proof

2.47 Carlsberg's gate is adorned with huge, carved stone elephants.

2.48 Elephant Beer.

2.49 / 2.50
- Elephant Beer—Carlsberg (Copenhagen, Denmark).
- Delirium Tremens (features a pink elephant)—Huyghe (Ghent, Belgium).
- Tusker—Kenya Breweries (Nairobi, Kenya).
- Also acceptable is the logo of Big Time Brewing (Seattle, WA).
  Other answers admissible with proof

2.51 Name two brewers who produce beers named Phoenix.

2.52 Bock beer as a style of beer often includes a picture of a goat on the label. Beer brewed for what seasonal event usually has baby chicks on its label? **2.53** Where is it brewed?

2.54 Name three brewing companies whose beer brands feature a goose on their labels.

2.55 Many brewing companies around the world have used African lions on their labels. Name a brewery that features a North American mountain lion, or cougar, on its label.

2.56 Name three or more breweries or beer brands that feature a North American bison on their labels.

(answers on the following page)

ANSWERS TO THE QUESTIONS ON PAGE 51:

2.51
- Cherry's Breweries (Waterford, Ireland).
- Mauritius Breweries (Mauritius).
  Other answers admissible with proof

2.52 Easter. **2.53** Throughout Scandinavia.
Other answers admissible with proof

2.54
- De Gaus Bierbrouwerij (Goes, Netherlands).
- Goose Island Brewing (Chicago, IL).
- Mishawaka Brewing (Mishawaka, IN).
- Wild Goose Brewery (Cambridge, MD).
  Other answers admissible with proof

2.55 Catamount Brewing (White River Junction, VT).
Other answers admissible with proof

2.56
- The entire product line of Bison Brewing (Berkeley, CA).
- Various products of Buffalo Bill's (Hayward, CA).
- Various products of Buffalo Brewing (Lackawanna, NY).
- Calgary Beer (Brewed by Molson in Calgary, Alberta, Canada).
  Other answers admissible with proof

2.57 Dozens of past and present beer labels have featured eagles on their labels. Name three or more beer brands that feature hawks or falcons on their labels. **2.58** Name the brewer of each.

2.59 Name three or more breweries whose products feature long-legged water birds such as egrets, herons, storks or cranes on their labels or logos.

2.60 Name three or more beer brands that feature bears on their labels. **2.61** Who brews them?

(answers on the following page)

ANSWERS TO THE QUESTIONS ON PAGE 53:

2.57 / 2.58
- Blackhawk Stout—Mendocino Brewing (Hopland, CA).
- Eye of the Hawk Ale—Mendocino Brewing (Hopland, CA).
- Red Tail Ale—Mendocino Brewing (Hopland, CA).
- Perigrine Pale Ale—Mendocino Brewing (Hopland, CA).
- Van Vollenhoven's Stout (Heineken-owned Van Vollenhoven Brewery, Amsterdam, Netherlands).

Other answers admissible with proof

2.59
- Bridgeport Brewing (Portland, OR).
- Crane River Brewpub (Lincoln, NB).
- Marin Brewing (Larkspur, CA).
- Mendocino Brewing (Blue Heron Pale, Hopland, CA).
- Rubbel Bernem / Brouwerij Bios (Ertvelde, Belgium).

Other answers admissible with proof

2.60 / 2.61
- Grizzly Canadian Lager—Amstel Brewery (Hamilton, Ontario, Canada).
- Bärenpils—Berliner Kindl (Berlin, Germany).
- The entire product line of Celis Brewery (Austin, TX).
- Golden Bear Dark Malt Liquor—Golden Pacific Brewing (Emeryville, CA).
- Gürten Bier—Gürten Brewery (Bern, Switzerland).
- Hamm's Big Bear Malt Liquor—Pabst Brewing (Milwaukee, WI and elsewhere).
- Boundary Waters Bock—James Page Brewery (Minneapolis, MN).
- Grant's Weis Beer—Yakima Brewing (Yakima, WA).

Other answers admissible with proof

2.62 Name a beer brand that features a loon on its label.
2.63 Who brews it?

2.64 Name three beer brands that feature a bull on their labels.
2.65 Name the brewer of each.

2.66 Name two brewing companies who produce beer with labels that feature pictures of flightless birds.

2.67 Name a beer brand that features a whale on its label. **2.68** Who brews it?

2.69 Name a brewery that featured a sea otter on its label.

(answers on the following page)

ANSWERS TO THE QUESTIONS ON PAGE 55:

2.62 Boundary Waters. **2.63** James Page Brewery (Minneapolis, MN).
Other answers admissible with proof

2.64 / 2.65
- Schlitz Malt Liquor—Stroh Brewery Company (Detroit, MI).
- Red Bull Malt Liquor—Stroh Brewery Company (Detroit, MI).
- Oxford Class Amber Ale—British Brewing (Baltimore, MD).
Other answers admissible with proof

2.66
- Emu: Swan Brewery (Perth, Australia).
- Ostrich: Featured on the labels Brouwerij [Brewery] t'lj (Amsterdam, Holland).
Other answers admissible with proof

2.67 Scrimshaw Pilsner Style. **2.68** North Coast Brewing (Fort Bragg, CA).
Other answers admissible with proof

2.69 Monterey Brewing (Monterey, CA).
Other answers admissible with proof

2.70 Many beer labels from around the world feature pictures of dragons. Name three or more *other* imaginary *animals* that have been featured on the labels or logos of other brands from around the world.

2.71 Also name the brewing company and/or product.

2.72 What discontinued American beer brand featured a Canadian Mountie on its cans and bottles?

(answers on the following page)

ANSWERS TO THE QUESTIONS ON PAGE 57:

2.70 / 2.71
- Anubis, the jackal-headed Egyptian god: The logo of the Oasis Brewery (Boulder, CO).
- Bigfoot or Sasquatch: Bigfoot Stout—Sierra Nevada Brewing (Chico, CA).
- Bear with deer antlers: The logo of Anderson Valley Brewing (Boonville, CA).
- Griffin: Corona Extra—Modelo (Mexico).
- Griffin: Griffin Brown Ale—Brasserie McAuslan (Montreal, Quebec, Canada).
- Griffin: The entire product line of Sprecher Brewing (Milwaukee, WI) features a griffin on the label.
- Kirin: Products of the Kirin Brewing Company (Japan) feature the Kirin from Chinese mythology, which is half dragon and half horse.
- Phoenix: Phoenix Beer—Cherry's Breweries (Waterford, Ireland).
- Phoenix: Phoenix Beer—Mauritius Breweries (Mauritius).
- Pegasus, the mythical winged horse: The logo of Drummond Brewing (Red Deer, Alberta, Canada).
- Unicorn: The products of Newman Brewing, Albany, NY
  Other answers admissible with proof

2.72 Drewry's (South Bend, IN).

2.73 Name three or more beers which picture the devil on their labels or make reference to him in their names. **2.74** Name the brewer of each.

2.75 What does the word "hell" mean when it appears on the label of a German beer?
a) Dark   b) Pale   c) Sinful

2.76 The label of what Belgian beer depicts Adam and Eve enjoying glasses of beer? **2.77** Who brews it?

ANSWERS TO THE QUESTIONS ON PAGE 59:

2.73 / 2.74
- Old Nick—Young & Company (London, England).
- Lucifer—Riva Brewery (Dentergem, Belgium).
- Devil's Brew—Devil Mountain Brewery (Benicia, CA).
- Satyr—De Block Brewery (Brussels, Belgium).
- Duivels Bier/Biere du Diable [Devil's Beer]—Vander Linden Brewery (Halle, Belgium).
- Bière des Sorcières d'Ellezelles—Voisin Brewery (Flobecq, Belgium).
  Other answers admissible with proof

2.75 b) Pale.

2.76 Forbidden Fruit.

2.77 De Kluis Brewery (Hoegaarden, Belgium).

3. MAKING BEER

3.01 What brewing company produces more beer than any other brewing company in the world?

3.02 Excluding American companies, what brewer produces the most beer?

3.03 True or False: Historically, people were brewing beer before they made wine.

3.04 What is India Pale Ale. **3.05** How did it originate?

3.06 What is "bock" beer?
   a) The last beer left in the bottom of the fermenting tank.
   b) A seasonal beer that appears in the spring or fall.
   c) A beer that originated in pagan Europe to be drunk at rituals involving the sacrifice of goats.

(answers on the following page)

ANSWERS TO THE QUESTIONS ON PAGE 63:

3.01 Anheuser-Busch (United States).

3.02 Heineken (The Netherlands).

3.03 True. Beer is one of humankind's oldest prepared foods, dating back 4,000 to 5,000 years or more.

3.04 India Pale Ale was developed by British brewers to be shipped to troops stationed in India.
3.05 It was highly hopped and higher in alcohol in order to preserve it on the long voyage.

3.06 b) Bock beer is a seasonal beer that appears in the spring or fall.

3.07 Malt liquor is not really "liquor" but is actually what type of beer?
a) Dry stout
b) Strong lager
c) Wheat beer

3.08 What is barley wine?
a) A wine made from barley instead of grapes
b) A malt liquor
c) A strong ale

3.09 Can "ale" be properly called "beer"?

3.10 Which of these varieties of beer is *not* a top-fermenting beer: porter, stout, lager, ale?

3.11 *Humulus lupulus* is the scientific name of what critical ingredient of modern beer?

(answers on the following page)

ANSWERS TO THE QUESTIONS ON PAGE 65:

3.07 b) Malt Liquor is a strong lager.

3.08 c) Barley wine is a strong ale.

3.09 Yes. Ale is just one of many *styles* of beer.

3.10 Lager is not a top-fermenting beer.

3.11 Hops.

3.12 In beer making, what is the name of the sweet liquid produced by mixing the malt grist with hot water prior to fermentation?

3.13 What is "white" beer?

3.14 The Latin name for lager yeast is adapted from the name of the brewery where it was first isolated in its purest form. What is the Latin name? **3.15** What is the name of the brewery? **3.16** Where is it located? **3.17** When did this event take place?

3.18 What Asian company is among the top five brewing companies in the world?

3.19 German Märzenbier, or "March beer," is traditionally consumed during what month?

(answers on the following page)

ANSWERS TO THE QUESTIONS ON PAGE 67:

3.12 Wort.

3.13 Beer brewed with wheat malt instead of, or in addition to, barley malt. In Germany it is called *weissbier* and in Flemish-speaking Belgium it is called *witbier*.

3.14 *Saccharomyces Carlsbergensis.*
3.15 Carlsberg.
3.16 Copenhagen, Denmark.
3.17 1847.

3.18 Kirin.

3.19 October.

3.20 What is altbier?
  a) Old beer
  b) Ale
  c) Beer designed to be consumed at high altitudes

3.21 What do Olympia, Washington, Golden, Colorado, and Burton-upon-Trent in England have in common besides the presence of breweries?

3.22 Today brewers use hops as a flavoring agent, imparting bitterness to beer. What were hops used for originally?

3.23 What state leads the United States in the production of hops?

3.24 What is the primary difference between beer stored in and served from kegs and beer stored in and served from casks?

3.25 Which of the following is the best color for the glass of a beer bottle? a) green b) brown c) clear **3.26** Why?

3.27 What is the process of kräusening?

(answers on the following page)

ANSWERS TO THE QUESTIONS ON PAGE 69:

3.20 Both a) and b) are correct. Altbier is German for beer of the old style, meaning it is beer brewed with top-fermenting, ale-type yeast rather than bottom-fermenting lager yeast.

3.21 Famous water that is particularly suited to beer making.

3.22 As a preservative, because the oils and resins present in hops prevent bacterial infection, although the Romans ate hops as a table vegetable.

3.23 Washington leads the United States in the production of hops.

3.24 The beer in kegs is stored and dispensed under pressure. The beer in casks is not pressurized and is drawn out by suction.

3.25 b) Brown.
3.26 Because it filters out the most light, and light can spoil the beer.

3.27 The addition of small amounts of unfermented wort (malt) to beer in the fermenting tank to provide carbonation in the secondary fermentation stage.

3.28 Does the German term "doppelbock" imply that the beer will have *twice* the alcohol content of regular bock?

3.29 What is "Diat" beer?
   a) A low-calorie beer developed in Holland for people on a diet
   b) A high alcohol, low sugar beer developed in Germany for diabetics
   c) A mild beer originally brewed by monks to be served at ecclesiastical conferences such as the Diat of Worms

3.30 What is kriek beer?

3.31 As a unit of measurement, how many gallons are there in a barrel of beer?

3.32 Where is the Senne Valley? **3.33** Why is it important?

3.34 What is a beer engine? **3.35** When was the first one patented? **3.36** By whom? **3.37** Where?

3.38 What is tesguino?

3.39 What are "finings" and what purpose do they serve in the brewing process?

(answers on the following page)

ANSWERS TO THE QUESTIONS ON PAGE 71:

3.28 No, not necessarily. Although the term "doppelbock" *does* mean "double bock," the beer does not usually have *twice* the alcohol, but it does have *more* alcohol.

3.29 b) A high alcohol, low sugar beer developed in Germany for diabetics.

3.30 Beer flavored with cherries.

3.31 31 gallons.

3.32 Southwest of Brussels, Belgium.
3.33 It is the home of Belgium's spontaneously fermented "lambic" beers, unique in all the world.

3.34 The suction pump that draws the beer up from a cask to be dispensed at a tap. **3.35** 1797. **3.36** Joseph Bramah. **3.37** England.

3.38 A beer produced from fermented corn once made by the Indians of Mexico and the American Southwest.

3.39 A substance made from the bladder of sturgeon added to beer during conditioning to clarify it.

4.
THE PEOPLE WHO MADE BEER FAMOUS

4.01 Who was the first home brewer to be elected president of the United States?

4.02 Name another American president who was a home brewer and who also brewed for commercial sale.

4.03 What famous women's college was founded in 1861 by a professional ale brewer?

4.04 Who was its founder?

4.05 Who was the first of the following to own a commercial brewery: Gerard Heineken, Henry Weinhard or Adolph Coors?

4.06 Who was second?

(answers on the following page)

ANSWERS TO THE QUESTIONS ON PAGE 75:

4.01 George Washington. (He had a brewhouse at Mount Vernon, and his recipe for beer is preserved in the New York Public Library.)

4.02 Thomas Jefferson. (He was also involved in a plan that would have established a US National Brewery.)

4.03 Vassar College (Poughkeepsie, NY).
4.04 Matthew Vassar.

4.05 / 4.06
1. Henry Weinhard (Portland, OR, 1862).
2. Gerard Heineken (Amsterdam, Netherlands, 1864).
3. Adolph Coors (Golden, CO, 1873).

4.07 / 4.08 Who were Anheuser and Busch?

4.09 / 4.10 What were the first names of these famous surnames in American brewing: Schlitz and Pabst?

4.11 When did Joseph Schlitz form Joseph Schlitz Brewing?
4.12 How long did he own it?

4.13 / 4.14 What were the first names of the men who founded these great Canadian brewing companies: Labatt and Molson?

4.15 / 4.16 What were the first names of the men who founded these great British brewing companies: Bass and Courage?

4.17 / 4.18 What were the first names of the men who founded these great Irish brewing companies: Guinness and Murphy's?

4.19 Who founded a brewery in 1872 on the present site of the Kennedy Center for the Performing Arts in Washington, DC?

(answers on the following page)

ANSWERS TO THE QUESTIONS ON PAGE 77:

4.07 Eberhard Anheuser was a plumbing supplier who ended up with a brewery when a creditor defaulted on a debt.

4.08 Adolphus Busch was a traveling salesman who married Anheuser's daughter Lilly in 1861. The rest, as they say, is history.

4.09 / 4.10 Joseph Schlitz and Captain Frederick Pabst.

4.11 Schlitz married the widow of his boss, August Krug, in 1874 and promptly renamed Krug's brewery after himself.

4.12 Unfortunately, Schlitz and his bride both drowned during a trip to Germany the following year.

4.13 / 4.14 John Labatt and John Molson.

4.15 / 4.16 William Bass and John Courage.

4.17 / 4.18 Arthur Guinness and James J Murphy (along with his brothers William, Francis and Jerome).

4.19 Christian Heurich.

4.20 What Old World ruler, accustomed to wine, said this after his first exposure to beer: "Who made you and from what? By the true Bacchus I know you not. He smells of nectar, but you smell of goat."

4.21 / 4.22 Who was Gambrinus and what was his real name?

4.23 Who said: "Once, during Prohibition, I was forced to live for days on nothing but food and water"?

4.24 What man, who later became president of the United States, briefly acted as a pitch man for Pabst Blue Ribbon Beer in 1954?

4.25 Who said: "Moderate use of alcohol does not clash with moral prohibition and only abuse is to be condemned"?

4.26 Who was the first woman to operate a brewery in Canada? **4.27 / 4.28** Where and when? **4.29** What is the present name of that brewery?

(answers on the following page)

ANSWERS TO THE QUESTIONS ON PAGE 79:

4.20 Julius Caesar

4.21 / 4.22 Gambrinus was the legendary "King of Beer." He was actually Jan Primus (Jan I) of Brabant (in Belgium) who lived in the thirteenth century.

4.23 W.C. Fields.

4.24 Ronald Wilson Reagan.

4.25 Pope John Paul II.

4.26 / 4.27 Susannah Oland and her husband John started brewing in 1867 at Dartmouth, Nova Scotia.
4.28 When he was killed in 1870, she took over the operation.

4.29 Moosehead Breweries, Ltd.

4.30 Who was the first American brewer to start his own railroad to deliver his beer?

4.31 During World War II, it was proposed that soldiers *not* be allowed to drink beer. Who said that this prohibition would be "harmful to the men in the service"?

4.32 / 4.33 Between 1940 and 1965 Philip Liebmann's Rheingold Beer sponsored the Miss Rheingold Contest in which as many as two million people in the New York, NY area voted for their favorite female face. However, the first and last Miss Rheingolds were actually picked by the brewery. Who were they?

4.34 Who was the last Miss Rheingold elected by popular vote?

4.35 / 4.36 / 4.37 No Miss Rheingold used her title as a springboard to stardom. Who were the three *losing* candidates in the Miss Rheingold Contest who went on to become film stars?

(answers on the following page)

ANSWERS TO THE QUESTIONS ON PAGE 81:

4.30 Adolphus Busch of Anheuser Busch.

4.31 General George C. Marshall, Chief of Staff of the US Army.

4.32 1940: Jinx Falkenberg (star of the films *Tex & Jinx* and *High Jinx*).
4.33 1965: Sharon Vaughn.

4.34 1964: Celeste Yarnell.

4.35 Tippi Hedron (1953).
4.36 Hope Lange (1954).
4.37 Diane Baker (1957).

4.38 Who is credited as having been the first man to brew beer in Australia? **4.39** In what year?

4.40 Who was elected president of the United States by promising to end Prohibition? **4.41** What year was he elected?

4.42 What ancient ruler called beer a "high and mighty liquor"?

4.43 Carling, O'Keefe, Labatt, Molson and Moosehead are all major Canadian brewing companies. What family name (not among these names) is linked to *two* of these brewing companies?

4.44 Who is the man at the right?
4.45 What brewing company did he represent?
4.46 In what year did he first appear?

(answers on the following page)

ANSWERS TO THE QUESTIONS ON PAGE 83:

4.38 John Boston.

4.39 1794.

4.40 Franklin Delano Roosevelt.

4.41 1932.

4.42 Julius Caesar.

4.43 Oland. There are two prominent lines of the family. One is responsible for the Moosehead Breweries, and the other was associated with Oland's Breweries, which became the Maritimes Region of Labatt Breweries in 1971.

4.44 Mr. Fourex.

4.45 Castlemaine Perkins Brewery (Brisbane, Australia).

4.46 1924.

5.
LEGENDS
AND LORE

5.01 / 5.02 What two regions of the world are generally recognized as the birthplaces of beer? **5.03** When was beer first brewed there?

5.04 According to legend, ancient Egyptians were taught to brew by which god?

5.05 Who was the Sumerian goddess of brewing after whom Fritz Maytag of Anchor Brewing named a special beer brewed in 1989?

5.06 In original English usage, what is the difference between a *brewer* and a *brewster*?

(answers on the following page)

ANSWERS TO THE QUESTIONS ON PAGE 87:

5.01 / 5.02 Egypt and the Middle East, particularily Sumeria and Mesopotamia.

5.03 Probably between 3,000 and 2,000 BC, but possibly earlier.

5.04 Osiris.

5.05 Ninkasi.

5.06 A brewer was a man who made beer, while a brewster was a woman who made beer. A woman who brewed beer might also be referred to as an "ale wife."

5.07 In old England, when the brewster—or ale wife—had brewed a new batch of beer, what symbol did she use to advertise this fact to the public?

5.08 / 5.09 What is the name and location of the world's oldest surviving brewpub? **5.10** What year was it founded?

5.11 Why did the Pilgrims land at Plymouth, MA in 1620 instead of farther south near New Amsterdam as was originally planned?

5.12 Guinness Stout originated in what city?
a) London
b) Liverpool
c) Dublin

5.13 What is the German word for brewpub?

5.14 What New York City brewpub is located in the building that once housed the National Temperance Society?

5.15 During World War II, the United States government reqired American breweries to set aside what percentage of their production for use by personnel in military service?
a) None
b) Five percent
c) Fifteen Percent

(answers on the following page)

ANSWERS TO THE QUESTIONS ON PAGE 89:

5.07 A broomstick posted on her house.

5.08 / 5.09 U Fleku on Kremenkova Street in Prague, Czech Republic.

5.10 1499.

5.11 According to legend, the *Mayflower* was running short of beer so the ship's crew decided to dump the Pilgrims at Plymouth in order to have enough beer for their trip back to England.

5.12 c) Guinness Stout originated in Dublin.

5.13 Hausbräuerei.

5.14 Zip City Brewing.

5.15 b) Fifteen percent.

5.16 Who established North America's first European-style commercial brewery? **5.17** Where? **5.18** In what year?

5.19 What is the oldest *existing* brewing company in the Western Hemisphere? **5.20** Who founded it? **5.21** When did it start brewing beer?

5.22 What's the oldest *existing* brewing company in the United States? **5.23** Where is it located? **5.24** When was it founded?

5.25 In Belgium, beer brewed by Trappist monks is highly prized. When was the last time beer was brewed by monks in the United States? **5.26** Where was it brewed?

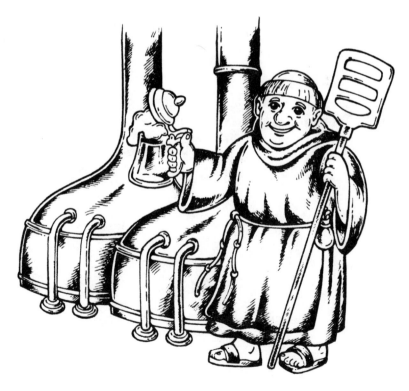

(answers on the following page)

ANSWERS TO THE QUESTIONS ON PAGE 91:

5.16 Alonso de Herrera.
5.17 Mexico.
5.18 1544.

5.19 Molson.
5.20 Founded by John Molson (in Montreal, Quebec).
5.21 1786.

5.22 Yuengling.
5.23 Pottsville, PA.
5.24 1829.

5.25 Between 1885 and 1899.
5.26 Beer was brewed by Benedictine monks at the St. Vincent Abbey at Beatty (near Latrobe), PA, (under the direction of Father Boniface Wimmer).

5.27 The microbrewery revolution of the 1980s literally revolutionized the beer scene in America. What was the name of the first micro-brewery? **5.28** Who started it? **5.29** When? **5.30** Does it still exist?

5.31 What was the name of the first microbrewery/brewpub opened in Canada? **5.32** What year did it open?

5.33 / 5.34 The two largest selling beer brands in Ireland are brewed at breweries named after someone's gate and someone's well. Which beers? **5.35** Whose well? **5.36** Whose gate?

(answers on the following page)

ANSWERS TO THE QUESTIONS ON PAGE 93:

5.27 New Albion Brewing (Sonoma, CA).
5.28 Jack McAuliffe.
5.29 Founded in 1977.
5.30 No, it closed in 1983.

5.31 Horseshoe Bay Brewer/Troller Pub (Vancouver, British
Columbia, Canada).
5.32 1982.

5.33 / 5.34 Murphy's and Guinness.
5.35 Murphy's is brewed at the Lady's Well Brewery (Cork).
5.36 Guinness is brewed at St. James Gate Brewery (Dublin).

5.37 What is, or who is, Figgy Sue?

Name the brewing companies whose ownership is associated with ownership of the following major league baseball teams:
5.38 St Louis Cardinals
5.39 Toronto Blue Jays
5.40 New York Yankees
(not currently, but in their heyday)

5.41 What is the best selling beer brand in the Western Hemisphere outside of the United States? **5.42** In what country is it brewed?

5.43 What city is home to the legendary, original Oktoberfest?

5.44 In what year was the first Oktoberfest held? **5.45** What event did it celebrate?

5.46 Who brews Rolling Rock beer? **5.47** What are three of the various explanations for the mysterious numerals "33" on the Rolling Rock bottle?

(answers on the following page)

ANSWERS TO THE QUESTIONS ON PAGE 95:

5.37 An early twentieth century concoction made with sugar, ginger and a gallon of beer to a pound of boiled figs.

5.38 St Louis Cardinals: Anheuser Busch.
5.39 Toronto Blue Jays: Labatt Breweries.
5.40 New York Yankees (not currently, but in their heyday): Colonel Jacob Ruppert's Ruppert Breweries.

5.41 Brahma. **5.42** Brazil.

5.43 Munich, capital of the German state of Bavaria.

5.44 1810. **5.45** The wedding of the crown prince of Bavaria.

5.46 Rolling Rock is brewed by Latrobe Brewing (Latrobe, PA).
5.47 Latrobe itself cannot remember why the 33 was put there in the first place because the product was introduced in 1939. However, among the most popular answers to the riddle are:
- Prohibition was repealed in 1933.
- There are 33 words on the back of the 12-ounce Rolling Rock bottle.
- There are 33 letters in the ingredients of Rolling Rock— water, malt, rice, corn, hops, brewer's yeast.
Other answers admissible with proof

5.48 What state in the United States has never had a brewery?

5.49 What state in the United States has had more breweries in its history than any other?

5.50 What state in the United States has more breweries than any other state today?

5.51 What Canadian province has more breweries than any other today?

5.52 When was canned beer introduced into the United States?
5.53 By which brewing company?

5.54 What is the origin of the word "Budweiser"?

5.55 Today, Anheuser Busch owns the trademark in the United States and much of the world for the Budweiser brand. Name three or more *other American* brewers who brewed beers called "Budweiser" in the past.

(answers on the following page)

ANSWERS TO THE QUESTIONS ON PAGE 87:

5.48 Mississippi.

5.49 Pennsylvania.

5.50 California.

5.51 Ontario.

5.52 1935. **5.53** Gottfried Brewing (Newark, NJ).

5.54 During the days of the Austro-Hungarian Empire, the important Czech brewing city of Ceske Budojovice was known by the German name Budweis, and beer from Budweis was called Budweiser. Today Budweiser beer (locally called Budvar) is still brewed in Ceske Budojovice, but it has nothing to do with the beer of the same name that is brewed in the United States.

5.55 • Bedford Brewing (Brooklyn, NY).
  • DuBois Brewing (Dubois, PA).
  • Franklin & Hayes Brewing (Pocatello, ID).
  • Leisy Brewing (Cleveland, OH).
  • Miller Brewing (Milwaukee, WI).
  • Joseph Schlitz (Milwaukee, WI).
  Other answers admissible with proof

5.56 When was the first pull tab can introduced? **5.57** By Whom?

5.58 In what year did canned beer first outsell bottled beer?

5.59 What is the origin of the six pack? Why not four, eight or ten?

5.60 Because of its size, Chicago should have been the major brewing center in the upper Midwest. What allowed Milwaukee to usurp this role?

5.61 In 1986, the Corona brand increased its market share by 160 percent, rising from an insignificant import to being the number two imported beer in the United States. What company brews Corona?
5.62 In what country is it brewed?

5.63 Guinness Stout originated in Ireland and is still also brewed in England and various Commonwealth countries. Was it ever brewed in the United States? **5.64 / 5.65** When and where?

5.66 What year did bottled beer outsell draft beer for the first time?

5.67 The Ballantine brand was known for its famous three rings. Each ring stood for an attribute of the beer. What were the three attributes? **5.68** When were the rings adopted?

(answers on the following page)

ANSWERS TO THE QUESTIONS ON PAGE 99:

5.56 / 5.57 It was patented by Alcoa Aluminum and first used by Pittsburgh Brewing in 1962.

5.58 1969.

5.59 In the 1930s the major brewing companies determined that six beer bottles was the maximum number that a *woman* would want to carry home from the market at one time.

5.60 After the fire of 1872 destroyed Chicago's breweries, the Milwaukee brewers (not the baseball team) "flooded" the market.

5.61 Modelo.
5.62 Mexico.

5.63 Yes.
5.64 / 5.65 1939-1954 in Long Island City, NY and 1949-1955 in Detroit, MI, Muskegan, MI and Oakland, CA.

5.66 1940.

5.67 Purity, Body, Flavor.
5.68 1879.

5.69 What American bottled beer was introduced in 1882 with a bit of ribbon tied around the neck?

5.70 What brewing company claims that its beer is brewed at night by mysterious, unseen gnomes?

5.71 True or False: Anchor Steam Beer, produced by Anchor Brewing Company of San Francisco, is so named because it is the result of a unique brewing process involving steam.

5.72 Where was the "longest bar in the world" located?
5.73 How long was it?

5.74 A large consignment of beer from what brewery went down in the sinking of the *Titanic* in April 1912?

(answers on the following page)

ANSWERS TO THE QUESTIONS ON PAGE 101:

5.69 Pabst Blue Ribbon. (The ribbon was blue, of course.)

5.70 La Chouffe (Achouffe, Belgium).

5.71 False. It was probably named for the puff of water vapor that escaped when a keg of beer was tapped.

5.72 The bar at the New Billburg (Rock Island, IL).
5.73 684 feet.

5.74 Bass & Company (Burton-upon-Trent, England).

5.75 What Amendment to the United States Constitution introduced Prohibition? **5.76** In what year?

5.77 What Amendment to the United States Constitution repealed Prohibition? **5.78** In what year?

5.79 In the depths of the Prohibition, when the idea of staying dry began to collapse, which state was first to repeal its Prohibition enforcement? **5.80** In what year?

5.81 / 5.82 In the United States, Prohibition was a federal affair. In Canada, it was enacted by the provinces. Which two provinces were the only ones *not* to establish *total* Prohibition?

5.83 After Prohibition ended in 1933, how long did it take for beer consumption to return to pre-Prohibition levels in the United States?
a) Seven months
b) Seventeen months
c) Seven years

(answers on the following page)

ANSWERS TO THE QUESTIONS ON PAGE 103:

5.75 The 18th Amendment.
5.76 1920.

5.77 The 21st Amendment.
5.78 1933.

5.79 Montana.
5.80 1926.

5.81 / 5.82 Quebec and British Columbia had laws that permitted the sale of wine and beer with various restrictions but they never totally banned them.

5.83 c) Seven years (1940).

5.84 What is the Reinheitsgebot?

5.85 / 5.86 When was the Reinheitsgebot law overturned and why?

5.87 Who are the "big six" brewers of Munich?

5.88 Which is the largest of the "big six" brewers of Munich?

5.89 In what country is the most beer consumed per capita?
a) United States
b) Belgium
c) Germany

5.90 Which of these countries is *not* among the top five beer-drinking nations, per capita?
a) United States
b) Denmark
c) New Zealand

5.91 What was Devonshire colic?

5.92 In what city was the original Canadian Ace Brewing Company located? **5.93** What years did it operate?

(answers on the following page)

ANSWERS TO THE QUESTIONS ON PAGE 105:

5.84 The German purity law of 1516 which required beer to be made of only water, hops, malt and yeast.

5.85 / 5.86 It was overturned in 1987 by the European Court—after 471 years on the books—because it prevented the sale within Germany of beer produced in other European Economic Community countries using chemical additives.

5.87 • Augustiner. • Lowenbrau.
  • Hacker-Pschorr. • Paulaner.
  • Hofbrauhaus. • Spaten.

5.88 Paulaner.

5.89 c) Germany.

5.90 a) United States.

5.91 Lead poisoning caused by the lead pipes used in the beer lines in English pubs until the mid-twentieth century.

5.92 Chicago, IL. **5.93** 1947-1968.

5.94 What is CAMRA? **5.95** What did it do? **5.96** When did it start?

5.97 What North American brewing company once operated a fleet of bright red, streamlined trucks that were designed by the same man who had built coaches for the Russian tsars? **5.98** What was the designer's name? **5.99** What year did they first appear?

5.100 What popular British ale is mentioned in the song "Thirty Days in the Hole" by the rock group Humble Pie? **5.101** What does the song say the beer can do?

5.102 In which of the following countries did Imperial Russian Stout originate:
a) Russia
b) Ukraine
c) England

(answers on the following page)

ANSWERS TO THE QUESTIONS ON PAGE 107:

5.94 The Campaign for Real Ale.

5.95 It was a consumer movement originating in Manchester, England that successfully helped to preserve traditionally-produced ales in the face of efforts by large brewers to fill the market with bland, mass-produced beer.

5.96 1972.

5.97 John Labatt Brewery (Canada).

5.98 Count Alexis de Sakhnoffsky.

5.99 1932.

5.100 Newcastle Brown.

5.101 "Newcastle Brown can sure smack you down."

5.102 c) Imperial Russian Stout was first brewed in the eighteenth century at the Anchor Brewery in Southwark, London, England. It was then exported to, and later brewed in, Russia.

5.103 Most people have heard of the Dutch surrealist painter Hiero-nymus Bosch (1450-1516). What internationally popular beer is brewed in his home town today?

5.104 Why did Louis Pasteur originally invent pasteurization?
   a) To kill deadly bacteria in milk and make it safe for children to drink
   b) To kill deadly bacteria in beer that had been causing epidemics in early nineteenth century Europe
   c) To kill active yeast in beer to halt the fermentation process

5.105 The nickname of a Holy Roman emperor was used as the name of a beer brewed by two related American brewing companies. The same name was also used as the code name for the German inva-sion of the USSR on June 22, 1941. What was the nickname?
5.106 Who was the emperor? **5.107 / 5.108** What were the two American brewing companies?

(answers on the following page)

ANSWERS TO THE QUESTIONS ON PAGE 108:

5.103 Heineken has a major brewing facility at s'Hertogenbosch in the Netherlands. (The name of the town means "the Duke's woods.")

5.104 Pasteur originated the pasteurization process to kill active yeast in beer to halt the fermentation process.

5.105 Barbarossa.

5.106 Frederick I (1123-1190), son of Frederick, duke of Swabia and the first of the Hohenstaufen line. He was a notorious beer drinker who drowned in Sicily.

5.107 Red Top Brewing (Cincinnati, OH) and **5.108** Atlantic Brewing (South Bend, IN).

CONGRATULATIONS!

Now that you've worked your way through *The Ultimate Book of Beer Trivia* and have become a Master of Beer Trivia just like us, we want to hear from you.

The second volume of *The Ultimate Book of Beer Trivia* is already in the works, and we're going to publish it as soon as we get enough questions.

If you'd like to see *your* favorite question used in the second volume of *The Ultimate Book of Beer Trivia*, send it to Bluewood Books, PO Box 460313, San Francisco, CA 94146.

If we use it, we'll include your name and hometown (unless you don't want us to, in which case, let us know) and we'll buy you a beer the next time we're in the same pub, tavern, bar or brewpub. So keep those cards and letters coming!

Cheers!